THE FIVE-MINUTE
CENTERPIECE

THE FIVE-MINUTE
CENTERPIECE

JANE NEWDICK

Conceived and produced by Breslich & Foss, London

Photographs by Jacqui Hurst
Illustrations by Marilyn Leader
Designed by Clare Finlaison
Original design by Lisa Tai
Printed and bound in Hong Kong

Published by Crown Publishers, Inc., 201 East 50th Street
New York, New York 10022.
A member of the Crown Publishing Group.

CROWN is a trademark of Crown Publishers, Inc.

Manufactured in Hong Kong

Library of Congress Cataloging-in-Publication Data

Newdick, Jane.
The five-minute centerpiece / Jane Newdick. — 1st ed.
p. cm.
Includes index.
1. Flower arrangement. 2. Table setting and decoration.
I. Title.
S3449.N35 1991
745.92—dc20 90-2424
CIP

ISBN 0-517-58226-0

10 9 8 7 6 5 4 3

Third Printing

Contents

THE FIVE-MINUTE APPROACH

Even in these days of fast food and eating on the run most of us sit down at a table to consume at least one meal a day in home surroundings. Given our hectic lifestyle these moments of relaxation become ever more important as oases of quiet, conversation, good food and company.

Flowers have an affinity with food. They help to make a table look welcoming and the food more delicious. They can be homely or fun, sophisticated or simple and they always show that someone cares. Just as many of us have no wish to spend hours cooking in the kitchen neither do we want to spend hours putting together elaborate flower decorations, at least not for day-to-day eating. So here in this book are plenty of table centerpieces which take five minutes or less to put together.

For formal and lavish entertaining the centerpiece has become very complicated and in some cases over fussy, combining not just flowers but a whole host of extra accessories. The ideas here are quite the opposite, even the ones designed for celebrations and special occasions. Expensive flowers and complicated ideas are not necessary to achieve stunning effects and you don't have to spend hours to create something worth looking at. Just bear in mind that flowers for tables should never dwarf the food and place settings, should not get in the way of the diners or smell so strongly that they overpower the foods and wine. The centerpiece should add a subtle emphasis to any color scheme you have created and should complement the fabrics, china, cutlery and glass on the table as well as providing something pretty to look at and possibly talk about.

The ideas range from a few simple flower stems standing in glasses to more elaborate textural arrangements worked into florist foam. They cover a range of seasons and events though

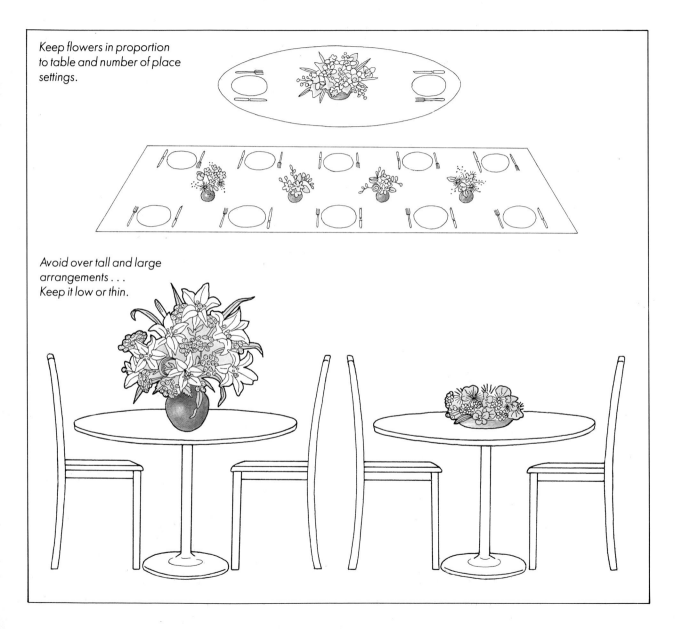

Keep flowers in proportion to table and number of place settings.

Avoid over tall and large arrangements . . .
Keep it low or thin.

most of the designs are interchangeable for different occasions. The book has been divided into sections such as Everyday Eating or Parties and Celebrations, but feel free to take ideas from anywhere to suit your mood and whatever ingredients you can get hold of.

PREPARATION AND CONDITIONING

The whole essence of a five-minute book is obviously speed in putting something together, but there is an important step you ought to take before doing anything else. Flowers which have been well prepared and conditioned will last very much longer than ones with no prior treatment.

You should therefore choose flowers from a good shop or stall where blooms will probably have been prepared and conditioned for you and buy things which are young and fresh. Material from your own garden will be young and healthy and simply cutting stems under water and using it straightaway will probably be enough to keep the material in good condition. If you do have time to condition your material ahead of time, then cut the stems and stand the flowers in a deep container with not too much tepid water and leave in a cool, dull place for several hours at least. This gives the stems time to take up plenty of moisture and plump up the plants' cells.

Before conditioning and arranging, always cut stems on a long slant using the sharpest available knife, scissors or secateurs. If you can do this under water, even better, as that way the cut surface never has a chance to dry out in the slightest. Always clean off any foliage and bits of stem which might sit below the water line in a vase or container. Left for a few days these bits and pieces will slowly rot and turn the water cloudy and unpleasant. You can buy a special cut-flower food which you dissolve into the water to keep the water fresh.

Flowers that have not been conditioned should be given a long drink.

Hammer the ends of woody stems to help them absorb water better.

Other tricks worth knowing about to keep arrangements fresh and long-lived include adding a drop or two of household bleach to the water or dropping a small piece of charcoal into the bottom of the container to keep the water sweet.

Some of the ideas in this book make use of small pots of growing plants, either foliage or flowering ones. Before putting these into an arrangement it is sensible to leave them standing overnight in a shallow bowl of water to be sure the soil is completely moist. Let the pot drain for a while before using it. Once put into a centerpiece it is sometimes difficult to keep the soil watered but if you pack the surface of the pot with moss this will help reduce moisture transpiration, and an occasional spray of water over the leaves will be all that is needed to keep the plant fresh. When the centerpiece is finished with, pot plants can be rested elsewhere, planted out into the garden if hardy or stood back in a light window or conservatory.

A few flowers need special treatment if they are to keep well. Stems which bleed such as ranunculus, poppies, euphorbia and hellebore should be seared over a flame or stood in boiling water for a few seconds to seal the ends.

Hard and woody stems of trees and shrubs should always be crushed or split before being arranged. This helps them to absorb water. Use a hammer, wooden mallet or a heavy rolling pin to crush stems on a wooden chopping board. Strip off extra foliage from shrubs such as lilac as it quickly wilts and spoils the effect of the flowers.

MATERIALS, CONTAINERS AND EQUIPMENT

Five-minute ideas don't require a whole cupboard full of special equipment and bits and pieces, but you will need a good pair of florist scissors or secateurs, some blocks of florist foam for some of the arrangements and thin rose wire on a reel.

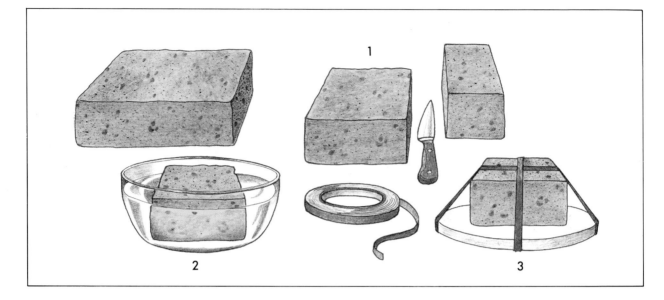

Fixing florist foam to base:
1 *cut and carve foam with a sharp knife*
2 *soak foam according to manufacturer's instructions*
3 *tape block to whatever base you are using.*

Many people are slightly frightened of using florist foam for the first time but it really is too useful a material to ignore, particularly for table arrangements. With a little experience you will find that you can be quite economical with it and it is possible to re-use it once or twice, though it does begin to lose its water-holding properties and the foam structure breaks down eventually.

While the foam is dry it can be cut with any sharp kitchen knife to fit any shape of container. The foam can be hidden down low in a shallow bowl or stood above the vase rim for taller arrangements. To fix blocks of foam onto a shallow or flat surface you will need a special tape which is available where you buy the foam.

Check with the manufacturer's instructions on how long to soak the foam in water. The newer types take just a minute or so and should not be oversoaked. Remember that the damp foam will leak water a little, especially when the flower stems are pushed into it, so always wrap the foam in plastic film or foil to protect anything that might get spoiled.

Containers can be bought, found and collected as you go but do buy suitable things when you see them and try to build up a stock of items which inspire their own ideas. Raid kitchen cupboards for utensils which can be pressed into service and don't reject jars or cans you might otherwise throw away. In many cases you can work straight into a block of foam placed on a plate or some metal foil so there is no need for a special container.

Centerpieces usually need low and shallow containers though tall, slender glasses are good for elegant single bloom arrangements. Baskets are extremely useful as they are very versatile and can be filled with foam easily and always look pretty and countrified when filled with flowers. For special occasions, utilise parts of a dinner service such as shallow vegetable dishes or soup plates which will give a nicely coordinated look to the whole table.

TABLE SETTINGS AND DETAILS

A centerpiece for a table has to be planned with the rest of the table in mind. Will there be food on serving dishes spread out across the table? Will people need to reach across and serve themselves? Will food be served away from the table leaving it free of clutter? Is it a formal occasion with many glasses, layers of cutlery and space needed for wine, sauces, small serving dishes and so on? The answers to these questions will determine the space and shape you will have for the flowers.

Next you may want to choose colors and a style or look to suit either china, tablecloth fabric or the general decor. Or perhaps the flowers are what will come first and everything else will follow and hinge round them. Once you have decided this, you can decide on flowers and foliage and containers.

Explore the possibilities of a wide range of container — shallow bowls, baskets, kitchen utensils, mugs and small stemmed glasses.

The season and weather may have a bearing on what ingredients are available for the centerpiece just as they will have on the food you serve, so be prepared to be flexible, see what looks good in the shop or market or choose whatever is at its best that day in your garden.

You will soon discover what looks good on a particular everyday table but ring the changes often so that the flower ideas don't get stale and go unnoticed. If you have a garden then pick from it often and display a few special blooms on the family table. It is a good way to keep up with the seasons and to see the changing moods of the garden at close hand.

Take trouble to add other details to the table as well as flowers. A range of different napkins to swap and change regularly is one of the best finishing touches. They don't have to be starched damask but large cotton squares look good and provide color and pattern which you can link up with the flowers you have chosen. Even if you normally use an uncovered table, it is a good idea to have a range of small cloths. You can use them to add atmosphere and detail to an otherwise bland surface and of course flowers will help bring the table to life.

MAKING IT WORK

Putting the centerpiece together should be very quick and easy if you have everything at hand and space to work in. Either choose to work in a kitchen or workroom where you can spread things out, or work straight on the table if the design is clean to do and won't spoil a polished surface or precious furniture. Always use just enough water and top up when necessary rather than risk a spill. You can also mist an arrangement with a fine water sprayer to keep the flowers looking crisp and fresh.

Color scheming is important but not such a difficult problem as it is often made out to be. If you are unsure about mixing colors successfully then be cautious and keep it simple. Choose

Use flowers throughout the table arrangement – individual posies, a long flower arrangement or a line of small pots.

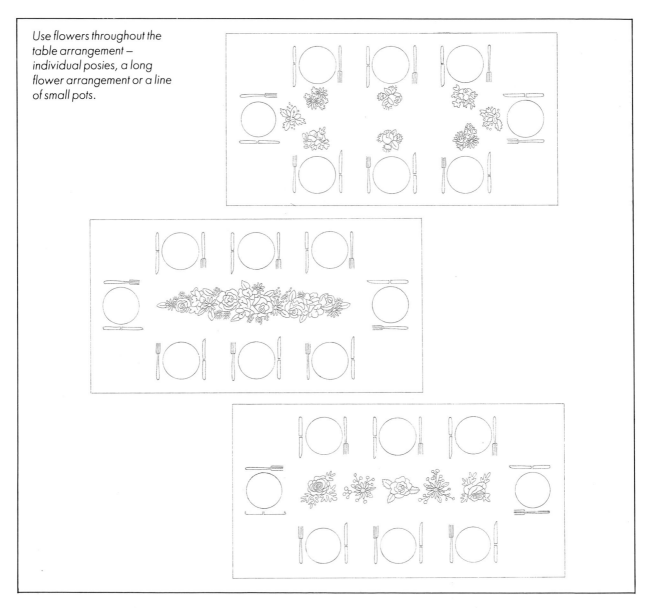

one color or tones of one color and stick to it. Many single color arrangements can benefit from a certain amount of green introduced through foliage. White or cream used alone always need some green added or a blue/grey green such as eucalyptus leaves to throw the plain white flowers into relief and give definition. When you mix more than one color, begin with safe combinations such as pale blue and apricot, or yellow, white and green. Try using many different pastel colors together like a summer herbaceous border, mixing pale pinks, blues, mauves, lemons and apricots. Add white or cream and green too to balance and dilute the other colors.

Keep the arrangement for seating people at the table in mind and make sure that the flowers will look good from everyone's viewpoint. This may seem very obvious but it is easy to work on an arrangement from one view only and end up with a definite right and wrong side.

If you have a long table arrangement, you can use flowers throughout rather than having a conventional centerpiece. Each person could have their own posy in front of their plate. After the meal the guests could take them as a memento or you could gather them together into a larger posy for your own pleasure. Another idea is to extend flowers along the length of the table using florist foam to make the base, or produce the same effect with a line of small pots. Another nice personal touch is to lay a bloom such as a rose on each side plate.

Your table centerpiece may take only five minutes to put together but it is pleasing if it lasts for more than one meal. Warm, well-heated rooms and strong daylight will hasten the flowers' demise but you can remove the arrangement to a cool place overnight and keep water freshly topped up to help keep flowers fresh. As some blooms fade ahead of others, remove them and replace with something else if you wish.

Many of the very long-lasting varieties are somehow the least exciting flowers. Chrysanthemums, carnations, gerbera are extremely useful and available all the year round but consequently are very over-used and a bit dull unless they are mixed with more unusual flowers and put into unconventional arrangements.

If you are able to grow and pick some of your own flowers for the house, then make sure to have a few basic and useful flowers which are hard to find in shops. Many of the summer annuals grown from seed can be gathered all through the summer months and thrive on being harvested, producing bloom after bloom if not allowed to seed.

Some of the best value and most useful annual flowers for picking are cornflowers, sweet peas, lavatera, zinnia, larkspur and marigolds. If you have more space and time then you can grow some of the perennial and biennial flowers which are also good for cutting, such as scabious, September flower, hellebore, phlox, dahlia, eryngium and sweet william, Shrubs, trees and rose bushes will provide flowers, seed-heads, fruits and seasonal color.

The other very valuable material which a gardener has is a choice of pretty and decorative foliage. Good foliage is scarce at the flower shop but the home gardener can produce all that is needed throughout the year.

1
FORMAL
OCCASIONS

LILIES WITH STONES

Ingredients
2 small containers
About 10 small pebbles
  in different colors
2 lily flower heads
2 ivy leaves

This idea could be said to offer an ideal solution to making a little go a long way. It relies on a smooth shiny surface to make reflections and the deep glossy black background certainly throws the pebbles and flowers into relief and makes a sophisticated, minimalist arrangement. Use a centerpiece such as this when the table is an uncovered shiny surface of wood, marble, plastic or lacquer.

Lilies are bought with very long stems and most people are loathe to cut them down but they take on a quite different style when used in this way and to get two blooms one stem will usually be enough. The *lilium auratum* hybrids have a wonderful heavy scent and even two blooms should fill a room with fragrance.

Collect a handful of pebbles from a beach walk or buy a few at a flower shop. Smooth rounded stones look stunning dropped into clear glass containers to secure flower stems and create underwater landscapes.

The small containers which hold the lilies are tiny earthenware straight-sided pots. They could also be miniature glass tumblers or metal cylinders or anything which has a plain surface and is the right scale.

1 *Clean the pebbles and fill containers with water.*

2 *Prepare the lilies by cutting the blooms off the main stem at the right height so that they sit neatly in the two containers.*

3 *Cut ivy leaves to same length as lilies and put one of each in the containers. Place a little way apart on table with pebbles round them.*

Violets in a basket

Ingredients
A small round shallow basket
A container to sit inside basket
A bunch of violets

This old-fashioned tea for two with madeira cake and Earl Grey tea has a centerpiece in just the right style. A simple bunch of velvety scented violets takes its cue from the bone-china tea service decorated with cottage garden pansies.

Violets have a short season during late winter and early spring but are quite irresistible displayed en masse in a flower shop. In Victorian England they were sold in small bunches on the city streets and even today they come very often edged with a frill of their own green leaves and tied carefully with thin string or twine.

Small and scented, violets make perfect table decorations for any meal and would look equally pretty with plain white china or any decorated set. They really are best left very simple and not mixed with other things so after buying them there is no more to be done except to re-cut the stems and give them a good long drink before standing the little bunch in a suitable container. Violets absorb moisture through their leaves and petals so a fine mist of clear tepid water refreshes them and looks pretty too.

1 *Find a suitable waterproof container which sits tightly into the basket. Fill it with water.*

2 *Cut about two thirds from violet stems. Shake to make bunch look fuller. Fill basket with violets letting a few hang over the edge.*

PINK POSY IN A PAPER FRILL

Ingredients
A paper doily
2 paper clips
6 pink hyacinths
6 white anemones
6 pink Angelique tulips
6 stems deep pink
  Peruvian lily
6 pale pink freesias
3 sprays deep pink
  chrysanthemums

A bunch or posy made in the hand is one of the quickest methods of making a flower arrangement. You could make several smaller posies and stand one beside or in front of each guest's place setting. Another variation on the same theme would be four or five matching posies ranged down the length of a long rectangular table.

Aim for a mixture of flower shapes and textures but keep all the blooms roughly to the same scale. Choose one solid flower as the center starting point and add flowers round it turning the bunch as you work, slowly building up rings of flowers until you have a neat and regular round bunch. While you work, fasten the stems with a rubber band or piece of florist wire to keep the bunch together securely. Finally trim the stems off neatly as low as you need for the posy to sit safely in the container and the cut edges to reach the water.

The flowers here are an early spring selection but this idea works well with blooms from any season though it is particularly suitable for all the scented flowers of spring and summer.

1 *Sort flowers and cut stems quite short. Split Peruvian lily and chrysanthemum sprays into individual stems.*

2 *Cut from edge of doily into center and remove a small circle. Overlap cut edges to make cone shape and secure with paper clips.*

3 *Tuck doily into a small tumbler. Begin posy with a hyacinth and build round it with anemones then tulips. Fasten with rubber band.*

4 *Add Peruvian lily, more hyacinths, freesias and chrysanthemums. Fasten posy again and stand in water-filled tumbler.*

RED ROSES AND EVERGREENS

Ingredients
½ standard block of
 florist foam
8–10 stems of red roses
10–12 stems of deep
 coral pink roses
A small bunch of pink
 genista
8 stems of pale pink
 spray carnations
A bunch of evergreen
 leaves such as choisya

Crisp white table linen and gilt-edged china demand a formal and sophisticated arrangement which is neat and controlled but richly colored and textured for plenty of impact.

In this case any color could have been chosen for the flowers as there was no color in the cloth or china which needed to be considered. The strong reds and corals of the roses make an important point of interest in an otherwise fairly bland table setting. The chances are that the color scheme for flowers in a setting such as this one would be based on what else is in the dining room, taking a key from curtains, carpets, walls or furniture.

Deep reds and greens always have a wintry feel to them but this idea could be successfully translated into a summer version using white or cream and pale green.

The arrangement sits low on the table and flowers and leaves touch the surface so no container is necessary except to protect the table from water. Simply stand the finished flowers on a small plate, tray or saucer which fits the foam so that it doesn't show beyond the flowers and spoil the effect.

1 *Sort flowers into variety groups. Soak foam until damp. Split or hammer rose stems and evergreen stems if woody.*

2 *Insert evergreen leaves to completely cover foam. Aim for a regular round outline and keep leaves quite low.*

3 *Add genista sprays regularly all over foam letting them arch outwards. Next add spray carnations spreading them evenly.*

4 *Insert coral roses as evenly spread as possible. Finish by putting bright red roses in the empty areas.*

PINK TULIPS AND RUE

Ingredients
A small metal mold,
   square or round
Florist foam
A bunch of rue
12 pink tulips
6 stems of cream freesia
10 stems of
   chincherinchees

Here pink tulips have been used in a rather unexpected way utilising their regular shapes to make a formal and organised arrangement reminiscent of a Victorian posy.

The starting point for the idea was a square fluted tin mold meant for baking sponge cakes or for cold desserts such as mousses. Molds of this kind make light and practical containers for all kinds of flower arrangements and their bright shiny surfaces add sparkle and reflection to the flowers.

You will have to use damp foam inside the mold to keep the flower stems in exactly the positions you choose. Once you have started to build up the rows of flowers you will find that this kind of arrangement is very simple to put together and you could make many variations on the same theme.

Make plenty of definition between each row of flowers by choosing contrasting colors or textures of leaves and flowers. Here the soft steely blue grey of the rue leaves makes a highly decorative filigree edge to the centerpiece. The addition of cream freesias means that there is a delicious fragrance to scent the room.

1 Cut a square of foam to fit into the container so that it reaches just below its top. Soak foam and push firmly into place.

2 Cut all stems quite short and lay in groups. Put a layer of rue round the edge plus a group in the center. Put one tulip inside this.

3 Make a circle of freesias round the rue in the center and space the chincherinchees round the outer edge inside the rue.

4 Put tulip stems neatly in a ring between the freesias and chincherinchees. Adjust amounts of flowers to size of container.

NERINES AND RANUNCULUS AND STEMMED GLASS

Ingredients
A small stemmed glass
  or china vase
Florist foam
A bunch of pale pink
  genista
A few stems of pink
  snowberry
6–8 stems of nerine
12–14 stems of pink
  ranunculus

A light and airy arrangement for a formal dining table. The multi-petalled pink ranunculus echo to perfection the shapes of the old-fashioned roses on the coffee cups. Instead of foliage, stems of delicate genista and sprays of pink-berried snowberry have been used.

This kind of design looks complicated to do but is in fact very simple if you work in the right sequence and aim for a balance of flowers and equal spacing between the larger blooms. The arrangement needs to be symmetrical and viewed from all angles if it is to be put in the center of a round table.

A container with a small stem works well and lifts the flowers off the table just enough to give an elegant feel combined with lightness. Glass is a good choice as its transparency reveals the flowers as the important part. A plain white porcelain stemmed vase would look fine too and practically disappears against a white tablecloth. Nerines are long lasting as a cut flower and are available from autumn to spring. Their pretty curled petals make delicate but sophisticated arrangements.

1 *Cut foam to fit the vase level with the surface. Soak foam and push into place. Prepare flowers and cut everything quite short.*

2 *Completely cover foam with the genista. Spread the snowberry stems evenly throughout.*

3 *Add the nerines round the vase and across the top of the arrangement. Insert ranunculus between nerines, and throughout the genista.*

2
EVERYDAY
MEALS

BOTTLES AND BLOOMS

Ingredients
6–8 small bottles
10–12 flowers,
  preferably different
  varieties

This idea is simple enough for anyone to copy and is one of the quickest arrangements in the book. It obviously looks very interesting when a variety of flower types is used but it could also be made by using one type of flower either in a mixture of container shapes or in a matching set.

Here the flowers are in a range of apricot and warm yellow tones which look good with the pale aqua of the old glass bottles. Small liqueur glasses or tiny tumblers would also make suitable containers for the flowers but try if possible to choose something which has a narrow neck to hold the flower head steady. Once you have made a collection of flowers in jars you can range them along the length of the table or stand them in a circle or a random group depending on the table setting.

At the end of the meal when everything is cleared away you can cluster the flowers together in the center of the table and rearrange the grouping at the next mealtime. If there is likely to be lots of stretching across the table to reach food and dishes it might be best to keep the small vases close together so that they don't get too much in the way.

1 *Match flowers to containers and carefully fill each bottle with water.*

2 *Measure stems against bottles. Cut stems to fit and hammer or split any woody stems. Put one or two flowers in each bottle.*

Eggcups and daisies

Ingredients
A set of eggcups
A matching plate or
    saucer
A bunch of daisies with
    some foliage
3 limes

Eggcups seem to be something that people often have in multiples tucked away in a cupboard and hardly ever used. They make superb little containers for small arrangements or single flowers and a group of several pots gives lots of scope for different groupings.

Plain white china eggcups here are matched sympathetically with fresh green and white daisies to make a little circle of flowers to surround a plate of limes. Choose flowers which are fairly light-weight as very heavy-headed blooms will tend to fall out of such small containers. Daisies are ideal as they can be tucked securely down into the cups with a few sprigs of their own pretty foliage.

Experiment by changing the final positions of the cups on the table. Make rows or lines spaced precisely apart or group them randomly to make a little landscape or forest of greenery and flowers. Eight is a good number to work with but use what you have from three to thirty! Keep the water level topped up daily as it will run out rapidly in a warm room in such a small container and daisies are quite thirsty little flowers.

1 *Sort out eggcups and fill each with water.*

2 *Cut the flowers from the main stem and cut a few sprigs of foliage the same size.*

3 *Put one or two leaves in each eggcup and add a daisy. Put two flowers in a few cups.*

4 *Polish the limes and arrange on the plate.*

BRILLIANT RANUNCULUS IN A LUSTRE JUG

Ingredients
A small wide-necked jug
  or mug
A bunch of ranunculus,
  12–15 blooms

A simple breakfast or teatime snack still deserves some flowers such as this clutch of ranunculus to cheer the table even if they are in the simplest container.

Few people can resist the charm of these old-fashioned many-petalled flowers which appear for sale in late winter and continue through to early summer. They last a long time in water slowly opening out fully to show off layer after layer of flimsy petals. Ranunculus need no special treatment but check before buying that they have strong undamaged stems and that the flower heads are not drooping.

In the summer months you could use garden marigolds or coreopsis or a handful of nasturtiums in the same lovely color range. The whole essence of a table decoration such as this one is simplicity and artlessness. It is enough just to enjoy the glowing colors and sturdy shapes of the flowers tucked into a treasured jug or mug and to add anything more, or to arrange the flowers in a more complicated way, would be quite out of keeping with the mood of a simple family meal.

1 *Sort out the flowers and fill the jug with water.*

2 *Split stems into single blooms and trim. Cut stems so that heads sit just above jug rim. Stand flowers one by one in jug.*

BLUE-AND-WHITE CHINA WITH NARCISSI

Ingredients
A block of florist foam
Foam tape
A shallow container
 such as a soup plate
6 stems of mimosa
6–8 small stems of
 evergreen leaves such
 as choisya or bay
12–15 multi-headed
 yellow narcissi

Spring flowers are some of the most cheerful blooms of the year. Many of them come in brilliant yellows with a fresh vibrant scent to match and make beautiful sunny arrangements with little effort on your part.

Mimosa with its evocative smell and strange fluffy flowers mixes happily with the multi-headed narcissi sold in generous bunches or picked from the garden. Blue-and-white patterned china has a special affinity with bright yellow flowers which contrast but never fight, reminiscent of blue spring skies and fields of yellow blooms.

Collect together a group of blue-and-white china and layer up some pieces by putting, say, a soup plate on a larger platter or a saucer on a plate. Mixing patterns and shapes is all part of the fun and all shades of blue seem to work together. This arrangement has been made using florist foam as it can be difficult standing heavy-headed daffodils on short stems in a shallow container. A little extra evergreen glossy foliage adds a touch of freshness and separates the solid yellow effect.

1 Cut a piece of foam to fit the plate leaving it slightly higher than the plate's edge. Soak foam and stand it in the plate.

2 Tape foam in place as shown. Sort out flowers and cut short enough to make a low covering to the foam.

3 Working round the dish begin to fill in with stems of mimosa being sure to hide the tape. Add evergreen stems to help cover foam.

4 Add the narcissi flower heads evenly throughout, filling any thin patches. Stand plate on a large platter or tray on the table.

LITTLE POTS OF GREENERY

Ingredients
7 helxine plants
7 small terracotta plant
  pots
Extra compost

This little green plant which comes in three different color variations has many and various names. Mind your own business, Baby's tears, Curse of Corsica or, properly, *helxine soleirolii* is a spreading nuisance if planted outdoors but contained in a pot makes a splendid houseplant if kept in light and airy conditions. The plain green variety is most common but the silver (*argentea*) and the golden-green version (*aurea*) are very pretty used with it.

Here the three varieties have been potted into old terracotta garden pots and stood in a circle to decorate a lunch table. The fresh green colors look light and summery against well-scrubbed antique pine and work well with simple pottery and homely food.

When the pots are not needed for the table they should be stood in a light but not too sunny window and kept moist all the time. Small chunks of the plant will propagate easily if planted up into new pots so that you can keep a fresh supply going throughout the year. Helxine is very well-behaved grown this way and will make a neat and rounded little mound of greenery which can be easily trimmed.

1 *If necessary, wash and scrub terracotta pots. Water plants a few hours before repotting so that they are quite moist.*

2 *Tap sides of pots with helxines and shake plants free. Press firmly into terracotta pots. Top up with extra compost as necessary.*

Check mug and plate with anemones

Ingredients
A matching plate and mug
A bunch of purple anemones, about 12 blooms

Few households have a large range of vases or flower baskets, but most have an assortment of mugs, cups and plates which can be put to use. Mugs make excellent vases and they can be used singly or grouped in a mass as a very effective centerpiece.

Choose mugs with strong colors or bold patterns and combine them with simple bright flowers especially kinds such as anemones that look good cut short and massed in a container alone and without foliage. Anemones are often sold in bunches of mixed colors but sometimes they are available in a single color which is more unusual and makes a bolder statement. Anemones last extremely well in water and are pretty at all stages from tight bud to fully-opened petals.

Here deep rich purple is boldly contrasted against a crisp black-and-white checked design on a mug and plate, all set off against plain white linen with mono-chromatic detailing and black and silver cutlery. Strong red flowers would look equally effective as would yellow, orange or shocking pink.

1 *For this arrangement you do not need the very long-stemmed anemones which are usually more expensive than shorter ones.*

2 *Separate blooms and trim off lower part of stems. Measure height of bloom against the mug to gauge the right size.*

3 *Simply put one flower at a time into the mug filling it evenly and quite densely. Stand mug in middle of plate and place in center of table.*

3
PARTIES AND
CELEBRATIONS

FLOATING CANDLES AND PINK ROSES

Ingredients
A large round shallow
   glass dish
10 floating candles or
   nightlights
10 roses
A few sprigs of dill
   flower

This simply stunning centerpiece for a party table relies for its effect on the magical combination of candlelight and pink roses. For this idea you will either need some candles which are specially designed to be floated in water or, as here, use colored nightlights inside a small metal case making them waterproof and able to float.

Several of these dishes set along a buffet table amongst food would look superb or just one could be used at a more formal set table for a celebratory meal or an unashamedly romantic occasion. The movement and warmth from the candles means that the whole arrangement is always gently on the move which makes it sparkle and glow prettily.

Any large flower head can be used to float amongst the candles. Try gardenias, camellias, lilies, gerbera. amaryllis, chrysanthemums and orchids. You can also split flowers up into petals and float these on the surface. The prettiest effect using this method is achieved by mixing a range of pastel colors such as lilac, pink, pale blue and cream.

1 *Fill glass bowl with water and gently place candles in it. Make sure there is enough water for them to float freely.*

2 *Snip off rose heads very close to end of stem. Cut dill flowers into many tiny florets.*

3 *Put rose heads and dill flowers to float amongst the candles. Light candles when everything is ready.*

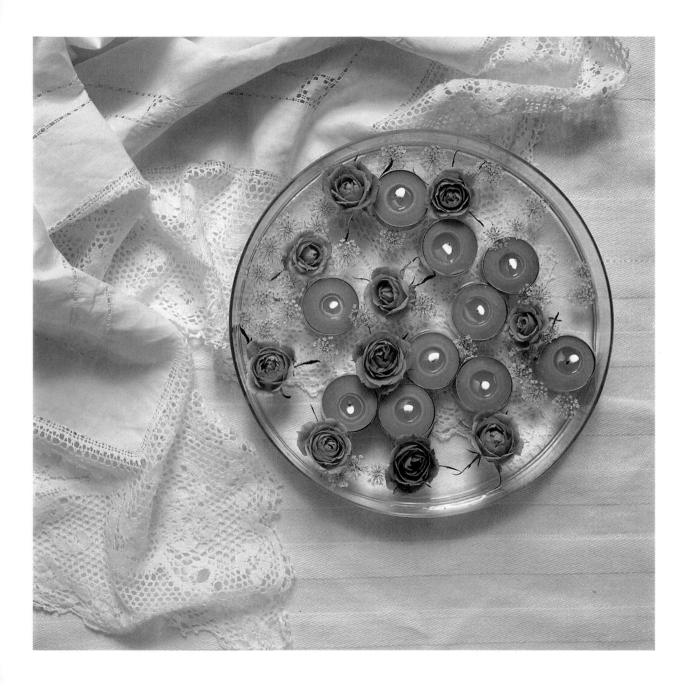

CHERRIES, CRANBERRIES AND AMARYLLIS

Ingredients
Florist foam
Plastic film
A shallow glossy basket
2 dark pink amaryllis
  blooms
A few deep pink
  Peruvian lily blooms
A selection of different
  fruits — cherries,
  lychees, mangoes,
  cranberries etc.
A selection of nuts —
  pecans, hazelnuts,
  almonds

This warm, glowing collection of fruit and flowers has a richness and depth of color which is further enhanced by the shining mahogany-colored woven basket. Here the choice of container is vitally important for the success of the whole arrangement. A matt-colored container in ceramic or glass would not have the impact which the basket lends to the fruit and flowers. A centerpiece like this can be used as a decoration and later raided at the dessert course for choice nuts and fruit to finish off a meal.

With a container in mind, shop carefully for fruit and nuts in a suitable color range and buy for looks as well as flavor. Wash and gently polish any fruit which would benefit from some added gloss and choose some of the less glamorous fruit to make a solid base to the pile.

If the arrangement is needed for only a very short time span it would be possible to dispense with the florist foam and simply tuck the flower heads in amongst the fruit where they will last a few hours.

1 *Collect together all the fruit and nuts and prepare the flowers cutting the stems very short.*

2 *Cut a small square block of foam and soak until wet. Wrap base of block in film and stand it in basket. Push amaryllis blooms into foam.*

3 *Insert Peruvian lily between the amaryllis. Add fruit using larger pieces first, with cherries, nuts and smaller fruits on top.*

ORANGES AND LEMON ROSES

Ingredients
A stemmed glass dish
A selection of small
  oranges, tangerines
  and kumquats
A bunch of orange,
  lemon or bay leaves
6 lemon roses
6–8 sprigs of winter
  jasmine

A warm and colorful mixture of fruit and flowers to be made when small tangerines and kumquats are in season. They are such decorative fruits in their own right that they need only a scattering of pale yellow rosebuds and a few deep green leaves and sprigs of winter jasmine to make a stunning centerpiece for a winter party.

Piling the fruit into a stemmed container creates a light and elegant effect though the same ingredients could work in a low plate or bowl. This chunky glass sugar basin makes a stylish but understated base to the fruit pyramid. If you own a larger glass or china stemmed dessert dish or comportere, adapt this design using larger-scale fruits such as oranges or lemons and limes, again with contrasting roses.

The flowers are simply tucked in amongst the fruit and will obviously wilt after several hours so this idea is definitely short term but will look fresh and sumptuous for a whole evening at least. Give the entire arrangement a light misting with cool water after you have assembled it to keep it as fresh as possible.

1 *Wash and polish all the fruit and prepare the flowers and leaves, cutting the stems short.*

2 *Pile the fruit into the bowl in a rough pyramid. Mix the different sizes of fruit quite randomly.*

3 *Tuck the leaves in amongst the fruit, holding them in place by the weight of a piece of fruit.*

4 *Push the roses and sprigs of jasmine into the spaces between fruit, spreading them evenly throughout the bowl.*

PINK AND WHITE TEXTURE IN THE ROUND

Ingredients

A large round shallow
bowl, glass or plain
china

A piece of small-mesh
wire netting

6 bunches at least of
different flowers

Wide, shallow containers can be quickly and
effectively filled by slotting flower heads into crumpled
wire netting inside the bowl. The wire holds the flowers
safely in place and makes a framework to help you
create a pattern of texture and color.

The flower stems should all be roughly the same
length but they can be chosen from many different
varieties. The version here has a controlled color range
from white to strong pink but it would work equally
well with a completely mixed palette of lots of strong
colors, mixing clashing reds, oranges, blues, yellows
and vivid pinks. The point would be lost if only one
color was chosen unless there was a great variety in
texture and size of the different blooms.

Aim for a dense mass of flowers to create a mixture of
textures but fill the wire in blocks of one type before
moving on to the next area. There is more impact with
patches of several flower heads rather than a random
spotty collection of single blooms.

1 *Crumple wire netting to fit
dish and fill with water. Cut
all stems very short. Push
stems of one flower variety
into a segment of wire.*

2 *Fill in the adjoining area
with a different flower variety
spacing flower heads out
equally.*

3 *Continue working across
the dish filling patches with
blocks of one variety until the
dish is covered.*

SUMMER POSY

Ingredients
A small straight-sided
  container
15–20 pink roses
A bunch of deep purple
  statice
A bunch of white
  September flower

A summer tea party to celebrate a special birthday has a pink, blue and white posy as a pretty centerpiece against the mellow pink of an antique quilt. The style is relaxed and countrified but also quite sophisticated with a mass of perfect pink rosebuds framed by deep lavender statice and tiny white starry September flower.

The method for putting a posy together is to make a bunch in the hand, building up quickly and fastening the stems securely. When a posy is finished it can simply stand in water in any container the right height and capacity and after the party it can be given to an honored guest as a charming present to take away.

Try to find the small, many-petalled roses which hold in bud and don't simply burst open and shatter as soon as they get warm or are put in strong light. Many more good varieties are being bred now including some with scent as well as small spray roses with several flower heads on one stem which are excellent for small posies and arrangements. Here the container is a simple modern square glass tank which shows off the centerpiece to perfection.

1 *Prepare all the flowers, stripping away leaves and thorns from rose stems.*

2 *Start with three pink roses and add statice and September flower round these.*

3 *Continue adding to the bunch turning it in your hand as you add flowers and keeping it round and even.*

4 *When you have used all the flowers, secure stems with a rubber band and trim stems to one length. Stand posy in container.*

ORCHIDS AND FLUTES

Ingredients

3 champagne flute
  glasses
3 yellow ranunculus
3 stems of orange
  orchids

A stylish way to make a few stems of flowers look spectacular is by using tall elegant champagne flutes and orange orchids with golden ranunculus. A trumpet-shaped glass or vase makes flower arranging simple. A single bloom or a small bunch of flowers lean gracefully with no help at all and the height makes for a sophisticated and light effect.

Stems of small-flowered orchids look exotic but are widely available and not expensive. They last very well in water and although they look stunning treated simply as here, they also mix well with other flowers for larger and more complicated arrangements. The brilliant yellow globes of the ranunculus are a key part of this centerpiece. The solid round shape contrasts with the twisty delicate orchid petals to give a sculptural effect. The silhouette of each stem and flower becomes the important part of the design.

Don't be tempted to add more flowers or foliage to an arrangement like this one — it is definitely a case of 'less is more'. The flower color has been chosen from the tablecloth and napkins and pulls the whole scheme together in harmony.

1 *Choose your colors to coordinate. Prepare flowers.*

2 *Clean stems of ranunculus, removing small leaves and branching stems.*

3 *Put a single orchid stem into each glass.*

4 *Add a ranunculus on opposite side of glass to balance the shape.*

4
ALFRESCO
MEALS

Cool white and aqua jug

Ingredients
Small wide-necked jug
6 stems of single white
   chrysanthemums
5–6 chincherinchees
Small bunch of white
   lace flower

White flowers always look fresh and cool and depending on the mood they can be ultra sophisticated or simple and countrified. Here they have been made into a posy and sit very happily in a dumpy aqua blue jug.

To be practical, flowers for outdoors should be put in down-to-earth containers which have a sensible low center of gravity. Low jugs and wide bowls make ideal vases as do lined baskets of all shapes and sizes. Flower pots, garden work baskets and even watering cans all make temporary homes for outdoor flowers and never look out of place in their alfresco setting.

The white flowers used for this centerpiece have plenty of their own natural greenery but if you choose flowers without foliage then add some extra fresh green leaves. All-white arrangements really do need the contrast of bright green; the darker tone sets off and outlines the all-white shapes which otherwise would disappear into an undefined mass of white.

1 *Prepare flowers and trim away leaves from chrysanthemums.*

2 *Cut stems to right length and put flowers in bunches of same type.*

3 *Stand bunches in jug working round the edge.*

Green and white in wire baskets

Ingredients
2 wire baskets
2 containers to fit inside
4 stems of viburnum
4 stems of white lilac
A bunch of cream
  genista
A bunch of white
  September flower

Two small decorative wire baskets, designed to be hung on a wall, stand back to back here on a table spread for a spring conservatory lunch. The color choice is a pale lime green mixed with white which makes a delectable color scheme against a strongly patterned pink-on-white Indian fabric. The table is set with white china and the food matches the mood — green salads, fresh fruit and crusty bread.

The pale green spheres of the snowball bush (*viburnum opulus*) are at their prettiest before they fully open to white; they are normally used in the green state with any foliage trimmed from the bare stems. Barely open sprays of white lilac plus a few stems of September flower and genista fill out the arrangement.

Be sure to prepare the stems of the lilac and viburnum carefully as they are both prone to wilting if the cut stem seals over. More often seen in large and elaborate displays, both shrubs also work well used in small-scale designs, where they can be seen in more detail.

1 *Prepare all flowers and stand containers in baskets.*

2 *Put tallish stems of viburnum in back of basket.*

3 *Add white lilac just in front of viburnum.*

4 *Next put genista in basket and fill out with little sprays of September flower.*

TWINING IVY IN POTS

Ingredients - for two pots
2 small terracotta pots
Florist foam
8 twigs
8 lengths of trailing ivy
Moss
Thin wire
Decorative ribbon

At first glance this arrangement looks like little ivy plants growing up twigs from terracotta pots. In fact the ivy is simply cut from long stems and pushed into damp foam hidden by moss. This may look quite complicated but it is really very quick to put together.

You will have to find a few dead twigs or buy some from a flower shop and the ivy can be some you find growing up a wall or tree or snipped sparingly from a house plant. The gauzy ribbon is an optional light-hearted finishing touch.

For an idea like this a pair is somehow far more satisfactory than a single pot. It does not take much longer to make two and they are then much more versatile when it comes to placing them. Aim for symmetry if you can but don't worry if the two are not precisely alike — part of their charm is the slightly crooked and home-made look which they have.

Ivy lasts surprisingly well treated in this way and the pot could stand out on a garden table for several days looking fresh and unusual. For a special occasion the nest of moss could be filled with tiny foil-wrapped sweets or presents.

1 Cut foam to fit pots. Soak and push into place.

2 Push 4 twigs into each pot locating them equally round pot and against the edge.

3 Push ivy stems into foam and twine each one round a twig. Press moss round bottom of stems to hide foam.

4 Tie tops of twigs together with small piece of wire. Tie ribbon round pot.

VINE WREATH AND BASKETS

Ingredients
2 small baskets
Florist foam
A small bunch of each of
these: eucalyptus,
rosemary, rue,
helichrysum lanatum,
lace flower, solidago,
Peruvian lily
Single chrysanthemum
1 vine wreath

With the use of herbs and the soft blue greens and lemon yellows this centerpiece has connotations of Mediterranean color schemes and scented *garigue*. Perfect for lazy summer lunches laid on rustic bare wood, the baskets and woven vine garland give a country feel.

You can use a garland to encircle other small collections of flowers. The center of the wreath could be filled with several small containers or one large shallow bowl which would be held securely and prettily encircled at the same time.

The two small baskets used here have been lined with tin foil to hold moisture in, not so important for an outdoor setting, but necessary for use on a vulnerable table surface or indoor furniture. Try to use some fresh herbs in the centerpiece to contrast with the flowers. Here sprigs of rosemary in flower and the rich glaucous green of rue add scent and texture to the overall effect.

1 Prepare and sort the flowers and foliage.

2 Cut foam to fit into each basket and soak. Line baskets with tin foil and put foam inside.

3 In one basket put bunches of eucalyptus and rosemary; put rue and helichrysum in the other.

4 Add white flowers: lace flower beside eucalyptus and chrysanthemum with rue. Add yellow flowers and place basket within wreath.

GYPSOPHILA AND SPOTTED SCARVES

Ingredients - for 2 jars
2 standard glass jars
2 cotton squares
2 rubber bands
A small bunch of
  gypsophila

Even the most relaxed meal of all — the picnic — needn't go without some kind of floral decoration. Here, the containers are empty jars, cleaned with tops removed, wrapped speedily in crisp square cotton handkerchiefs or scarves in bright unsophisticated patterns. Gingham checks, spots or stripes would look just as good but be sure to choose something bold and bright and eye-catching.

Gypsophila is fresh, light and airy and weighs very little so that it is a good choice of flower for an arrangement which is likely to be precariously propped on a less than flat tablecloth. It combines well with the spotty scarf design and is summery and simple at the same time.

Another choice of flower might be a single white daisy or annual chrysanthemum but don't choose anything which is too sophisticated or exotic. A group of these jars would make a splendid centerpiece for a garden buffet table or barbecue party. Groups of three jars together would have maximum impact.

1 *Clean the jars and stand each one in the middle of a cotton square.*

2 *Bring the fabric up, gathering it around the mouth of the jar. Hold it tight in one hand.*

3 *Use a rubber band to hold fabric in place round neck of jar. Split gypsophila into small sprigs.*

4 *Fill jar with water and put sprigs of flowers inside making a full but open bunch.*

Anemones and red apples

Ingredients
3 red apples
A bunch of mixed
anemones

Here, rosy-red apples have been hollowed out to make containers for small bunches of vibrant mixed colored anemones. If a layer of apple flesh is left intact throughout, the fruit are perfectly waterproof. A group of these cheerful decorations would look lovely on a table laid outdoors or in a sunny garden room or conservatory. Here the brilliant golden-yellow cloth and Provençal fabric napkins add even more punch to the vivid color scheme and would be bold enough to work in the strongest sunshine.

A variation on this theme might be shiny green apples holding yellow and white flowers or pale yellow-green apples with pink blooms. Other fruits and vegetables can also be used in this way to make unusual containers. All the small squashes and pumpkins are ideal for hollowing out as are melons and large winter root vegetables.

Finish off the table setting with bowls of more red apples for eating and choose brightly colored cutlery to complement everything. Top up the water level in the apples from time to time as obviously the reservoir is quite small.

1 *Polish the apples and if necessary shave a thin sliver from base to make them stand securely.*

2 *Cut a slice from the top and then hollow out the center of each apple leaving a thick enough wall of flesh to hold water.*

3 *Fill apples with water. Cut anemones very short and divide them evenly between apples.*

5
SEASONS AND
TRADITIONS

CHRISTMAS REDS AND GREENS ON TARTAN

Ingredients
A block of florist foam
Tin foil
A bunch of mixed
  evergreens e.g. ivy,
  euonymus, holly
5–6 stems of holly
  berries
12–15 stems of miniature
  red roses

Tartan fabrics and ribbons in the traditional seasonal colors of red and green have become a Christmas classic and make a superb festive table covering. A centerpiece which is bold enough to compete with this strong pattern and color is made here from plain and variegated evergreen foliage, glossy red holly berries and tiny brilliant scarlet roses.

The whole arrangement has been made using a piece of damp foam with no container so that the flowers and leaves appear to sit straight on the table. This centerpiece is made in the round but it could easily be adapted to suit any size and shape of table and would look superb made in a long low shape to run down the length of a long refectory table. Simply cut or join blocks of foam to make the shape you want and build the arrangement onto this structure.

Try to find a good mixture of different types of evergreen foliage if you can. Here, the variegated euonymus and ivy add some light and sparkle to what would otherwise be a rather dark sombre green.

1 Cut a square block of foam and soak until damp. Prepare leaves and flowers. Cut piece of tin foil to fit as mat under foam.

2 Start to cover foam with short stems of mixed evergreens.

3 Completely cover foam with greenery.

4 Add stems of holly berries evenly throughout greenery. Finally add the roses between berries.

POTS OF YELLOW IRIS

Ingredients
A large oval bowl
Bun moss to cover
   surface
Several pots of *iris
   danfordiae*

Small pots of growing *iris danfordiae* are often available in spring to plant in the garden or to use as an indoor decoration. These pretty scented iris break through the soil surface with very little leaf and open out on short sturdy stems shading into greenish yellow at the base of the petals. Grouped together they make a pool of spring sunlight and once they have finished flowering indoors they can be planted in a well-drained border or tub outside to flower another year.

You can buy the corms in autumn and plant small pots yourself but it is a lot easier to leave it to a professional grower who will manage to get his whole crop flowering all together. For a short-term centerpiece the small plastic pots can simply sit in a larger container which is then finished off with a thick layer of fresh bun moss.

Other small bulbs which would be suitable for this treatment would be deep purple *iris reticulata*, all the early winter crocus, *iris histroides*, grape hyacinth, and miniature narcissi species.

1 *Pick over the moss and spray with water to dampen.*

2 *If bowl is not waterproof, line it with tin foil which will also raise height of pots if necessary. Stand pots in bowl.*

3 *Pack in all the pots, then put a layer of moss over pot surfaces to hide soil and pots.*

SPRING FLOWERS AND MOSS ON MARBLE

Ingredients
A small piece of marble
as a base
Fresh bun moss
China egg or similar
container
A few smooth pebbles
10–12 stems of scented
narcissi
4–6 twigs of hazel
catkins
A few ivy leaves

This centerpiece is like a small landscape for a tabletop. It combines little pale lemon-scented narcissi and hazel catkins on a bed of damp green moss. The half china egg simply emphasises the season and the whole thing looks fresh and cool on a slab of grey and white marble. The flowers are tucked into the other half of the china egg which is set down in the moss. This idea could be copied without the egg, as any shallow tin or dish could be used as a water container and disguised in amongst the moss.

Spring flowers always look marvellous given this treatment which works beautifully for tiny bulbs such as snowdrops, scillas and the earliest iris and crocus. Primroses and violets seem perfectly at home tucked in a bed of moss as do all the small flowered narcissi.

As summer grows nearer, flowers seem to get bigger and stronger and don't respond quite so well to this very understated treatment, so save this design for early spring days when any flower, however small and insignificant, is a welcome sight after a long grey winter.

1 *Prepare flowers and cut stems very short. Spray moss to dampen.*

2 *Stand egg on marble and fill with water. Lay moss all round egg to enclose it.*

3 *Put pebbles in place amongst moss and stand other half of egg in position. Begin to fill egg with narcissi.*

4 *Continue until all the narcissi are in place. Add the hazel twigs and finally tuck about 4 ivy leaves in moss.*

BERRIES IN A BASKET

Ingredients
A small basket with a
  handle
Tin foil
Florist foam
6–8 stems of variegated
  ivy
Thin florist wire
2 small pumpkins or
  squashes
10–12 well-colored
  leaves
A bunch of rose hips
A bunch of pyracantha
  or similar berries
2 stems of *iris
  foetidissima* berries or
  similar

This is a centerpiece for the time of year when there are
bright shiny berries and richly colored leaves to use.
The pale green squash are very much part of the
complete design but you could use another shape or
color or even a different fruit or vegetable.

Berries are plentiful for only a relatively short time, so
make the most of them as soon as the first rose hips
begin to appear and ripen at the end of the summer
through to early winter when the frost or greedy birds
strip the stems before you can.

Make sure to line a basket well before putting the
damp foam into it or find a waterproof container which
fits neatly inside the basket and then put the foam
inside this.

An arrangement such as this would look pretty at any
style of meal from everyday to a full-scale celebration.
It would look especially good used with sturdy, simple
china and chunky cutlery. A fine polished wood surface like the oak one here completes the warm and
mellow feel.

1 *Cut tin foil to fit and line
basket. Soak foam and cut
to fit inside basket.*

2 *Put a long stem of ivy in
foam close to handle and
wind it round handle, fixing
with wire if necessary. Do
same for other side.*

3 *Put small bunches of
different berries and leaves
into foam working round
basket. Twist a sprig of ivy
round stem of squashes.*

4 *Add more bunches to
basket aiming to cover foam
completely.*

LEAVES AND SQUASH

Ingredients
A decorative dinner
  plate
2 squash
2 colored leaves
A small bunch of dried
  hydrangea

The varied shapes and subtle colors of squash are worth exploiting as decorative additions to autumn centerpieces. Here pale yellow squashes are simply standing on a vine-entwined plate with a few sprigs of soft green dried hydrangea and some bronzey rust-colored leaves.

There is absolutely no skill required to put this together but to make a successful decoration you must begin with a harmonious collection of items. The starting point here was the plate which suggested using leaves; the two squashes were then picked out for their interesting shapes and different sizes. The little florets of hydrangea pull everything together and add another color note which is unusual and unexpected.

It would be possible to make many different versions of this idea in the autumn when there are all kinds of fruits and vegetables in abundance. This color scheme is quite restrained but you could make wonderfully brilliant arrangements using oranges, reds and golds.

Make use of autumn leaves to decorate bowls and baskets of fruit or platters of cheese while in the summer you could use fresh vine or strawberry leaves.

1 *Choose squash of different shapes and sizes.*

2 *Put the squash in position on the plate. Cut the hydrangea into small florets.*

3 *Lay the leaves between the squash and add pieces of hydrangea to overlap leaves.*

HYDRANGEAS, NUTS AND GILDED LEAVES

Ingredients
A plate
About 3 dried
 hydrangea heads
20–25 pecan nuts in
 shells
2–3 dried magnolia
 leaves or similar
Gold paint

This centerpiece has been designed with Christmas and winter meals in mind though it is quite subtle with its glitter and could work for any time of year. There is very little effort involved in putting the arrangement together and you could make it either larger or smaller to suit your table.

The pecans in their shells need no added decoration, nor do the richly colored dried hydrangea heads, but one of the dried magnolia grandiflora leaves has a light covering of gold paint. Try to find bronze powders which come in several different shades and can be mixed into a transparent medium. They give a far superior effect to ordinary gold paints and lacquers and are not wasteful as you mix only the amount you need. The one used here is a rich yellow-gold powder which is echoed by the gold thread running through the elaborate design of the tablecloth fabric.

The plate you choose to hold the display is important and should have the same warm red tones as the hydrangea heads.

1 *Choose decorative shiny nuts in their shells and good deep red hydrangeas if possible.*

2 *Using a small paintbrush or natural sponge, paint top surface of magnolia leaves. Leave to dry.*

3 *Put hydrangeas close together on plate first.*

4 *Put pecans on opposite side of plate. Tuck one gold leaf under nuts at edge of plate and lay one leaf up the other way.*

INDEX